Freedom Song

Words by Emma Farry

with paintings by Ewan McDougall

First published in 2018 by Be Loved Press Ltd.
86 Waitea Rd, Muriwai Beach,
Auckland 0881, New Zealand

Text: © 2018 Emma Farry
Artwork: © 2018 Ewan McDougall

Designed by: Kyle Ranudo
Edited by: Geoff Walker

All rights reserved. No part of this publication
may be reproduced or transmitted in
any form or by any means without prior
permission in writing from Be Loved Press.

For further copies or comments, please email:
me@emmafarry.com

Printed in China through Asia Pacific Offset

ISBN: 978-0-473-41013-1

For Mark, Kahlil & Rafiq

Preface

When I was 25 years old I worked as a researcher on a television documentary that looked at the real-life stories of those living in the kind of poverty and violence depicted in the iconic New Zealand movie 'Once Were Warriors'.

One of the film's stars and I visited people in their homes and asked them about their lives. I will never forget one young woman's story, although her name and face I can no longer recall.

She told us in a strangely detached way about her baby's death at the hands of her boyfriend, and although I was holding back my own tears, she seemed somehow unmoved by the tragedy she described.

The sadness of this woman's life and the lack of love that it illustrated affected me deeply. I woke in the middle of the night after our interview and wrote the first draft of what was to become 'Freedom Song'.

The poem has been a kind of touchstone
for me ever since.

My husband and I were living in the West Village in Manhattan when the planes flew into the towers on September 11 2001.
Our lives were turned upside down, our apartment was covered in white dust and our city became a restricted war zone.

Again I turned to the words of this poem to try to make sense of what had happened.

'Freedom Song' returned with us to New Zealand and as we started our family and our new business it stayed in the background of our lives. I read it to my two boys when they were old enough to understand its message and I knew one day it would make its way out into the world.

In 2010 while we were living near Dunedin in the South Island of New Zealand I saw Ewan McDougall's art at Gallery de Novo and I knew I had finally found the perfect artistic collaborator for 'Freedom Song'.

At this point the poem was edited and extended thanks to the wise guidance of publishing consultant, Geoff Walker.

I was lucky once again to find the talented designer Kyle Ranudo, whose vision brought all the elements of the book together.

I am excited to offer 'Freedom Song' to the world at a time when we could all benefit from the simple truths of the spirit. I offer it in the same way it was offered to me, with unconditional love and hope for the future.

Emma

Home is
Heaven
JMcD
2002

There's not enough love
to go around,

I flap my small wings
but I can't leave the ground.

wots it to ya
EMD

There's not enough love
to go around,

Uneasy silence
the only sound.

There's not enough love
in this small blue-green sphere

To take us forward –
take us anywhere.

PINK
HAIL
E McD

There's a lack of love,
and the lack is deep,

There's a lack of love
and a lot of sleep.

3 Nihilists EMcD.

Millions of people are
sleeping right through,

Not knowing that love is
what they must do.

parched
wilderness

Afraid of moving
but scared to keep still,

Afraid of our beauty
and the strength of our will.

CIOUS

Afraid that the leaders
do not know the score,

Afraid of the wisdom
that lies at their core.

Neb
E MᶜD

Afraid of the darkness
and scared of the light,

Afraid of the wonder
and depth of our sight.

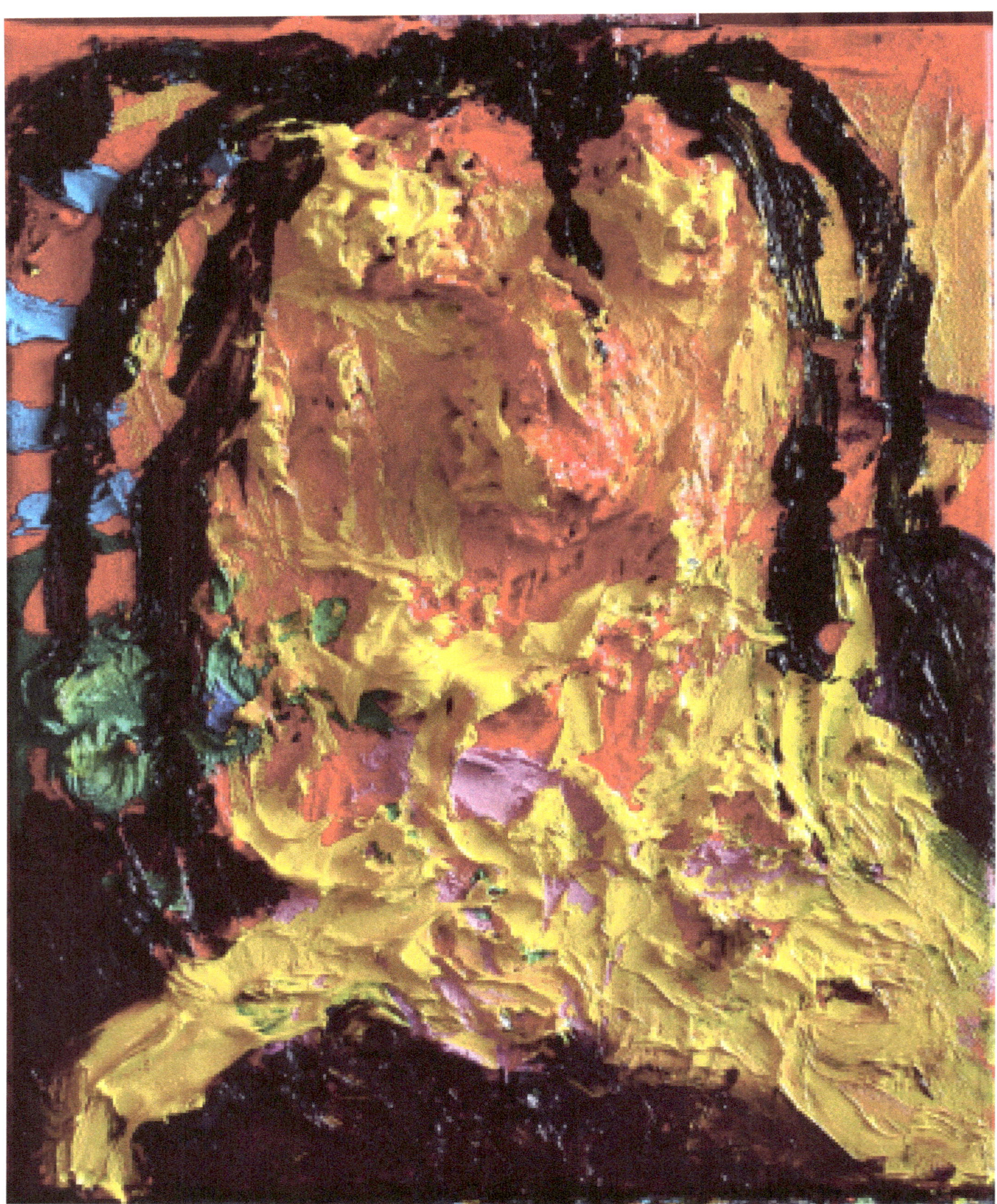

Afraid that the race
is all there is left,

Afraid that we'll die
before becoming the best.

Afraid that all of it
ends in the grave,

Afraid that our whole lives
are lived out as slaves.

Revelations 16:13
EMc D

Caught up forever,
in another one's web.

Caught up in prisons,
inside our own heads.

Scared to dissolve it
and scared to give in,

We spend all our days
holding tight from within.

WILD ideas
EMcD

But that which we're holding
deserves to be free,

Because that which we're holding
divides you and me.

When we can let go
of our ego-bound dreams

And wave goodbye smiling
to unevolved schemes,

Brain Explosion

Then the curtain between us
would be ripped right in two

And you would be me
and I would be you.

MUSOS CLUB
EMcD

And because there is nothing
between us anymore

We'd see that the same flame is
at each one's core.

And safe in this knowledge
true love would abide,

United and balanced
our spirits could glide.

Astrophysicist
Chess Grandmaster
Raconteur
Gets sticks

Not gliding off slowly
to some faraway space

But back on this earth,
grounded right in this place.

Happy New Year
yeah
EM'0

Together in love
and finally free,

We can worship our god
in whatever we see,

In a goat and a rock
and a whale and a dog,

In a newt and a lake
and a bird and a frog.

Walk The Walk
E McD.

We can learn from our mother,
from nature, the earth,

We can celebrate women
and children and birth.

We can look at God's face
in our fathers and boys,

Make room for our ancestors,
reclaim our joys.

And if we make friends
with dear Jesus the son,

Or Buddha or Shiva,
the Prophet, the one.

No one will judge us,
and no one will care,

Our hearts will be open,
our minds remain clear.

We'll accept that together
on this plentiful sphere

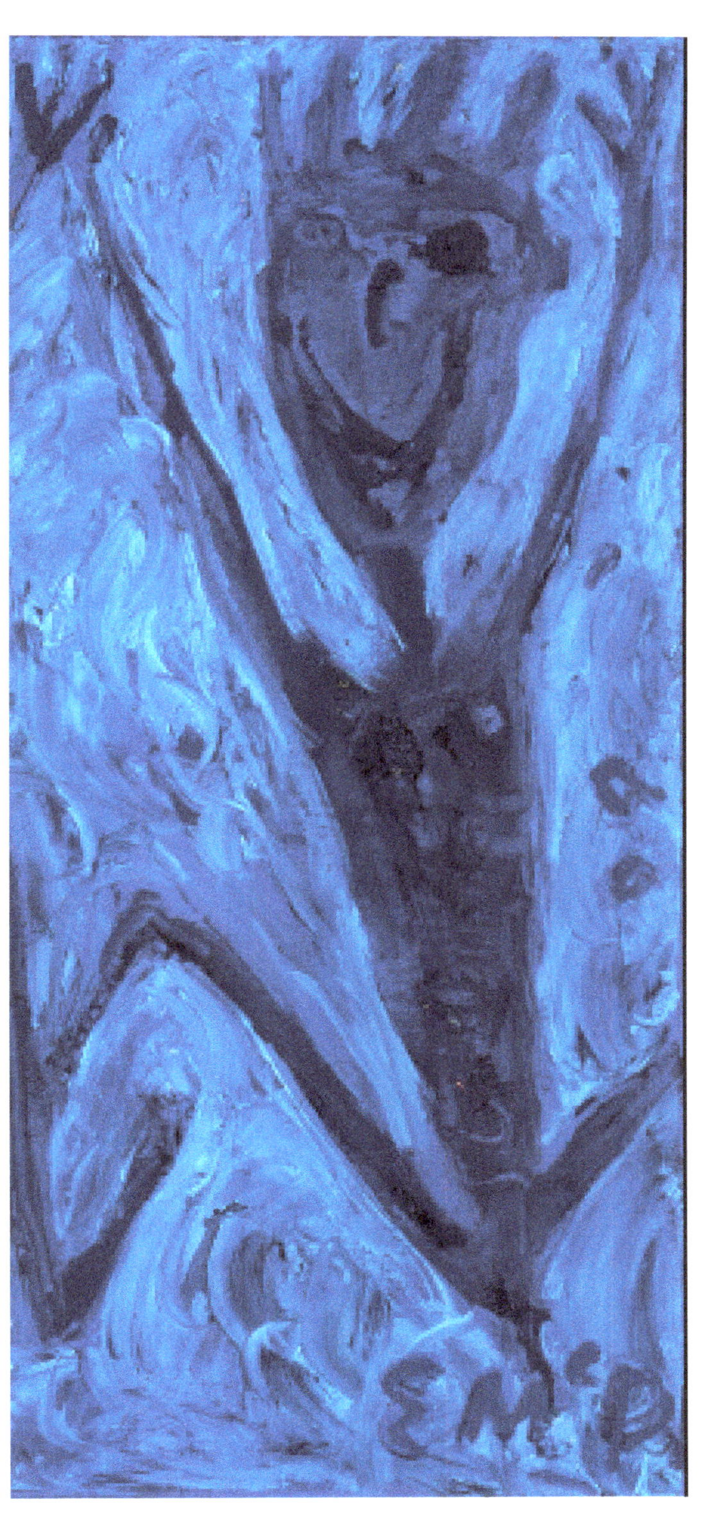

We can make a true home,
we can face down our fear.

Fukawi

We'll embrace ourselves deeply,
acceptance will rise,

And we'll know to rejoice when
one of us dies.

And the fear of each other
that reigns on the earth

Will dissolve in our hearts
with this simple rebirth.

We'll rejoice that there'll be
enough love to go around,

So I'll flap my small wings

Heaven

And with love
leave the ground.

Emma Farry

EMMA FARRY is an award-winning author.
Her titles, Beloved, Be Love and Freedom Song
encourage self-awareness, connection and
compassion.

She teaches meditation and mindfulness at
the Auckland Women's Centre and Shakti
International, a not for profit group for
empowering migrant women.

Emma received a post-grad diploma in
journalism from Canterbury University and
has worked in several countries as a journalist
and television researcher. Her first novel was
published in New York in 2001.

Ewan McDougall

EWAN MCDOUGALL was born in Wellington, New Zealand. His family later moved to Oamaru where he was educated at Waitaki Boys High School and taught by Colin Wheeler. Ewan attended Otago University while also working in freezing works and drumming in rock bands. He gained an Honours Degree in Political Studies in 1971. He worked at Otago University as an academic before travelling widely.

In 1983 he married his partner Sarah in Perth, Western Australia, and returned to New Zealand and after being admitted to Queen Mary Hospital in Hamner Springs for treatment for addiction in 1988, he began to paint full-time.

McDougall has had eighty-five solo exhibitions and has exhibited in New Zealand public galleries and internationally.

In 2003, Ewan showed in Southern Heat in the Dunedin Public Art Gallery and in February, 2015, the touring solo show Fun and Fury was hosted by the Tauranga Art Gallery. This exhibition was hosted by Te Manawa in April – August, 2016.

In 1994 he exhibited in Penzance and St. Ives in Cornwall.

Ten years later he exhibited in the Sydney Art Show with Gallery 2021.

In 2005 McDougall exhibited in London with the prestigious Rebecca Hossack Gallery, as well as showing in the Chelsea Art Show and the London Art Fair. That year he also exhibited at Arte Imagini Gallery in Cremona City, Italy.

In 2006 he showed in Color Elefante Gallery in Valencia, Spain. And in May, 2012, Ewan exhibited with other New Zealand artists in Chelsea, New York City.

In 2017 Ewan showed in the Dunedin Sister City Exhibition on the Yu Yuan Gardens Gallery in Shanghai and in the Brighton Arts Festival, UK.

Ewan is married to playwright Sarah McDougall and has three children: Melissa, Paul, and William.

Paintings
in order of
appearance

Page 6

Home is Heaven, **2013** 76cm x 76cm oil on canvas

Page 16

Day 40: Wilderness **2001,** 71cm x 56cm oil on canvas

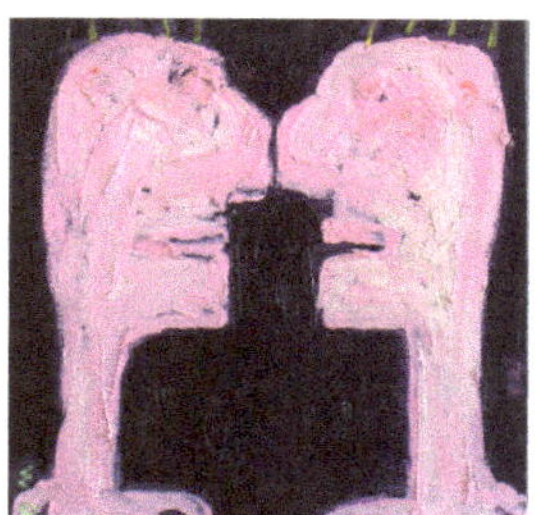

Page 8

Wots It To Ya, 2014 50cm x 40cm oil on board

Page 18

You're Vicious, 2014 102cm x 160cm oil on canvas

Page 10

Bloody Greenies II, **2011** 76cm x 76cm oil on canvas

Page 20

Nebuchadnezzar Stag Do, 2017 60cm x 92cm oil on canvas diptych

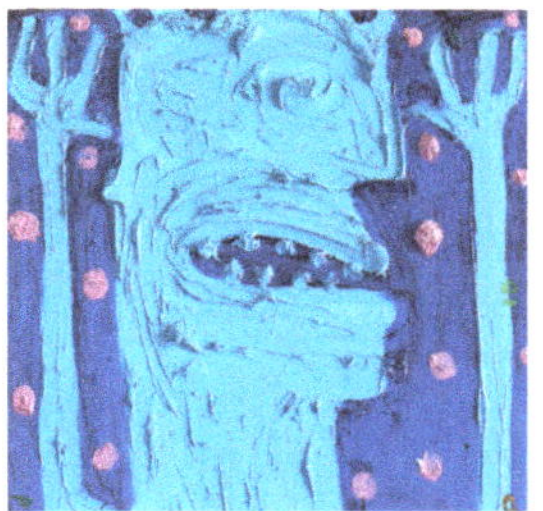

Page 12

Pink Hail, 2010 51 x 41cm oil on canvas

Page 22

Head of Nebuchadnezzar, **2017** 30cm x 26cm oil impasto on canvas

Page 14

3 Nihilists, 2005 58cm x 40cm oil on board

Page 24

Revelations 16:13, **2015** 102cm x 160cm oil on canvas diptych

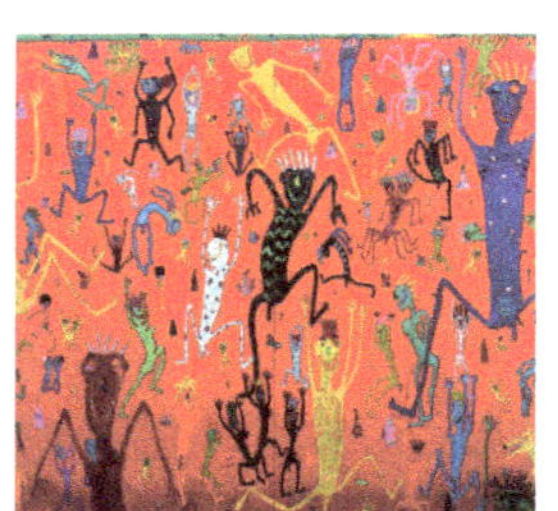

Page 46
Blue, Blue Feeling,
2009 78cm x
100cm
oil on canvas

Page 48
Up th' Creek, **2016**
120cm x 150cm
oil on canvas

Page 50
Plastered 11, **2016**
30cm x 26cm
oil on canvas

Page 52
*I'm in with the In
Crowd,* **2005**
136cm x 184cm
oil on canvas

Page 54
Heaven, **2001**
80cm x 120cm
oil on board

First published in 2018 by Be Loved Press Ltd.
86 Waitea Rd, Muriwai Beach,
Auckland 0881, New Zealand

Text: © 2018 Emma Farry
Artwork: © 2018 Ewan McDougall

Designed by: Kyle Ranudo
Edited by: Geoff Walker

All rights reserved. No part of this publication
may be reproduced or transmitted in any form
or by any means without prior permission in
writing from Be Loved Press.

For further copies or comments, please email:
me@emmafarry.com

Printed in China through Asia Pacific Offset

ISBN: 978-0-473-41013-1

Be Loved Press

belovedpress.co.nz

www.ingramcontent.com/pod-product-compliance
Lightning Source LLC
Chambersburg PA
CBHW042051030726
47599CB00019B/2445

9 780473 410131